My Favorite Raw Food Recipes Book

A collection of the most awesome, vitality-full & delicious recipes that I have found or created so far

Journal Easy

© 2014

www.journaleasy.com – making journal writing effortless

Name:

Ingredients:

Preparation:

Comments:

Name:

Ingredients:

Preparation:

Comments:

Name:

Ingredients:

Preparation:

Comments:

Name:

Ingredients:

Preparation:

Comments:

Name:

Ingredients:

Preparation:

Comments:

Name:

Ingredients:

Preparation:

Comments:

Name:

Ingredients:

Preparation:

Comments:

Name:

Ingredients:

Preparation:

Comments:

Name:

Ingredients:

Preparation:

Comments:

Name:

Ingredients:

Preparation:

Comments:

Name:

Ingredients:

Preparation:

Comments:

Name:

Ingredients:

Preparation:

Comments:

Name:

Ingredients:

Preparation:

Comments:

Name:

Ingredients:

Preparation:

Comments:

Name:

Ingredients:

Preparation:

Comments:

Name:

Ingredients:

Preparation:

Comments:

Name:

Ingredients:

Preparation:

Comments:

Name:

Ingredients:

Preparation:

Comments:

Name:

Ingredients:

Preparation:

Comments:

Name:

Ingredients:

Preparation:

Comments:

Name:

Ingredients:

Preparation:

Comments:

Name:

Ingredients:

Preparation:

Comments:

Name:

Ingredients:

Preparation:

Comments:

Name:

Ingredients:

Preparation:

Comments:

Name:

Ingredients:

Preparation:

Comments:

Name:

Ingredients:

Preparation:

Comments:

Name:

Ingredients:

Preparation:

Comments:

Name:

Ingredients:

Preparation:

Comments:

Name:

Ingredients:

Preparation:

Comments:

Name:

Ingredients:

Preparation:

Comments:

Name:

Ingredients:

Preparation:

Comments:

Name:

Ingredients:

Preparation:

Comments:

Name:

Ingredients:

Preparation:

Comments:

Name:

Ingredients:

Preparation:

Comments:

Name:

Ingredients:

Preparation:

Comments:

Name:

Ingredients:

Preparation:

Comments:

Name:

Ingredients:

Preparation:

Comments:

Name:

Ingredients:

Preparation:

Comments:

Name:

Ingredients:

Preparation:

Comments:

Name:

Ingredients:

Preparation:

Comments:

Name:

Ingredients:

Preparation:

Comments:

Name:

Ingredients:

Preparation:

Comments:

Name:

Ingredients:

Preparation:

Comments:

Name:

Ingredients:

Preparation:

Comments:

Name:

Ingredients:

Preparation:

Comments:

Name:

Ingredients:

Preparation:

Comments:

Name:

Ingredients:

Preparation:

Comments:

Name:

Ingredients:

Preparation:

Comments:

Name:

Ingredients:

Preparation:

Comments:

Name:

Ingredients:

Preparation:

Comments:

Name:

Ingredients:

Preparation:

Comments:

Name:

Ingredients:

Preparation:

Comments:

Name:

Ingredients:

Preparation:

Comments:

Name:

Ingredients:

Preparation:

Comments:

Name:

Ingredients:

Preparation:

Comments:

Name:

Ingredients:

Preparation:

Comments:

Name:

Ingredients:

Preparation:

Comments:

Name:

Ingredients:

Preparation:

Comments:

Name:

Ingredients:

Preparation:

Comments:

Name:

Ingredients:

Preparation:

Comments:

Name:

Ingredients:

Preparation:

Comments:

Name:

Ingredients:

Preparation:

Comments:

Name:

Ingredients:

Preparation:

Comments:

Name:

Ingredients:

Preparation:

Comments:

Name:

Ingredients:

Preparation:

Comments:

Name:

Ingredients:

Preparation:

Comments:

Name:

Ingredients:

Preparation:

Comments:

Name:

Ingredients:

Preparation:

Comments:

Name:

Ingredients:

Preparation:

Comments:

Name:

Ingredients:

Preparation:

Comments:

Name:

Ingredients:

Preparation:

Comments:

Name:

Ingredients:

Preparation:

Comments:

Name:

Ingredients:

Preparation:

Comments:

Name:

Ingredients:

Preparation:

Comments:

Name:

Ingredients:

Preparation:

Comments:

Name:

Ingredients:

Preparation:

Comments:

Name:

Ingredients:

Preparation:

Comments:

Name:

Ingredients:

Preparation:

Comments:

Name:

Ingredients:

Preparation:

Comments:

Name:

Ingredients:

Preparation:

Comments:

Name:

Ingredients:

Preparation:

Comments:

Name:

Ingredients:

Preparation:

Comments:

Name:

Ingredients:

Preparation:

Comments:

Name:

Ingredients:

Preparation:

Comments:

Name:

Ingredients:

Preparation:

Comments:

Name:

Ingredients:

Preparation:

Comments:

Name:

Ingredients:

Preparation:

Comments:

Name:

Ingredients:

Preparation:

Comments:

Name:

Ingredients:

Preparation:

Comments:

Name:

Ingredients:

Preparation:

Comments:

Name:

Ingredients:

Preparation:

Comments:

Name:

Ingredients:

Preparation:

Comments:

Name:

Ingredients:

Preparation:

Comments:

Name:

Ingredients:

Preparation:

Comments:

Name:

Ingredients:

Preparation:

Comments:

Name:

Ingredients:

Preparation:

Comments:

Name:

Ingredients:

Preparation:

Comments:

Name:

Ingredients:

Preparation:

Comments:

Name:

Ingredients:

Preparation:

Comments:

Name:

Ingredients:

Preparation:

Comments:

Name:

Ingredients:

Preparation:

Comments:

Name:

Ingredients:

Preparation:

Comments:

Name:

Ingredients:

Preparation:

Comments:

Name:

Ingredients:

Preparation:

Comments:

Name:

Ingredients:

Preparation:

Comments:

Name:

Ingredients:

Preparation:

Comments:

Name:

Ingredients:

Preparation:

Comments:

Name:

Ingredients:

Preparation:

Comments:

Name:

Ingredients:

Preparation:

Comments:

Name:

Ingredients:

Preparation:

Comments:

Name:

Ingredients:

Preparation:

Comments:

Name:

Ingredients:

Preparation:

Comments:

Name:

Ingredients:

Preparation:

Comments:

Name:

Ingredients:

Preparation:

Comments:

Name:

Ingredients:

Preparation:

Comments:

Name:

Ingredients:

Preparation:

Comments:

Name:

Ingredients:

Preparation:

Comments:

Name:

Ingredients:

Preparation:

Comments:

Name:

Ingredients:

Preparation:

Comments:

Name:

Ingredients:

Preparation:

Comments:

Name:

Ingredients:

Preparation:

Comments:

Name:

Ingredients:

Preparation:

Comments:

Name:

Ingredients:

Preparation:

Comments:

Name:

Ingredients:

Preparation:

Comments:

Name:

Ingredients:

Preparation:

Comments:

Name:

Ingredients:

Preparation:

Comments:

Name:

Ingredients:

Preparation:

Comments:

Name:

Ingredients:

Preparation:

Comments:

Name:

Ingredients:

Preparation:

Comments:

Name:

Ingredients:

Preparation:

Comments:

Name:

Ingredients:

Preparation:

Comments:

Name:

Ingredients:

Preparation:

Comments:

Name:

Ingredients:

Preparation:

Comments:

Name:

Ingredients:

Preparation:

Comments:

Name:

Ingredients:

Preparation:

Comments:

Name:

Ingredients:

Preparation:

Comments:

Name:

Ingredients:

Preparation:

Comments:

Name:

Ingredients:

Preparation:

Comments:

Name:

Ingredients:

Preparation:

Comments:

Name:

Ingredients:

Preparation:

Comments:

My Favorite Raw Food Books & Resources

www.journaleasy.com – making journal writing effortless

My Favorite Raw Food Books & Resources

www.journaleasy.com – making journal writing effortless

My Favorite Raw Food Books & Resources

My Favorite Raw Food Books & Resources

www.journaleasy.com – making journal writing effortless

www.ingramcontent.com/pod-product-compliance
Lightning Source LLC
LaVergne TN
LVHW011713060526
838200LV00051B/2891